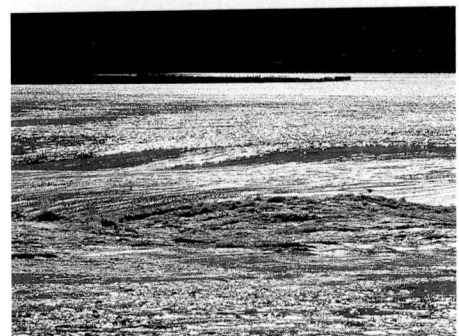

DESTINATION
FUNDY TRAIL
NEW BRUNSWICK

George Fischer

Claude Bouchard

Introduction by Mary Majka & David Christie

Copyright © George Fischer and Claude Bouchard, 2002

All rights reserved. No part of this book may be reproduced, stored in a retrieval system or transmitted in any form or by any means without the prior written permission from the publisher, or, in the case of photocopying or other reprographic copying, permission from CANCOPY (Canadian Copyright Licensing Agency), 1 Yonge Street, Suite 1900, Toronto, Ontario, M5E 1E5.

Nimbus Publishing Limited
P.O. Box 9166, Halifax, NS   B3K 5M8
(902) 455-4286

Graphic Design: Graphic Detail Inc., Charlottetown, PEI

Front Cover: Through an arch in a rock at Hopewell, the sun's warm morning rays transform the light and provide nourishment to the many species of plants and algae abundant in the Bay of Fundy.
Title Page: The St. John River becomes a raging torrent of swirling, foaming water at Reversing Falls in Saint John as the river fights with the incoming Bay of Fundy tides.
Back Cover: A sudden burst of sunlight makes the reddish-brown mud flats near Johnson's Mills glisten.

Printed and bound in Canada

National Library of Canada Cataloguing in Publication

Fischer, George, 1954-
Destination Fundy Trail, New Brunswick / George Fischer, Claude Bouchard ; introduction by Mary Majka & David Christie.

ISBN 1-55109-398-7

1. Fundy, Bay of—Pictorial works. 2. New Brunswick—Pictorial works. I. Bouchard, Claude, 1950 Dec. 29- II. Title. III. Title: Fundy Trail.

FC2495.F85F58 2002   917.15'3'00222
C2002-901355-0   F1044.F85F58 2002

We acknowledge the financial support of the Government of Canada through the Book Publishing Industry Development Program (BPIDP) and the Canada Council for our publishing activities.

Acknowledgements :

George Fischer
I would like to express my gratitude to Verdiroc Development Corporation and principals Harold, Cary, Kevin and Eric Green for their enthusiastic support and commitment to the production of this magnificent book on the Bay of Fundy. Verdiroc's awareness of the environment and its long-term vision for the future has helped save fragile ecosystems like the Bay of Fundy for future generations to enjoy. By supporting this book, Verdiroc has set an example as a Canadian company committed to making Canada—and New Brunswick—a better place to live.

Claude Bouchard
Special thanks to Anne and Gilles of Brault Design in Montreal for the map of the Bay of Fundy, and to the two wardens of Fundy National Park for their help when needed.

Photos by George Fischer on pages—title, vii, 1-6, 9, 11, 14, 17, 18, 23, 26, 28, 29, 32, 35, back cover.

Photos by Claude Bouchard on pages—front cover, iii, v, viii, x, xii, 7, 8, 10, 12, 13, 15, 16, 19-22, 24, 25, 27, 30, 31, 33, 34, 36.

Back cover photo of George Fischer by Dolores Breau.

Back cover photo of Claude Bouchard by George Fischer.

To Mother Nature for its nourishment of my soul
- George Fischer

To Him, and to Linda my wife. When I was fifteen,
I went to nature to find myself. I found him...
- Claude Bouchard

Destination Fundy Trail

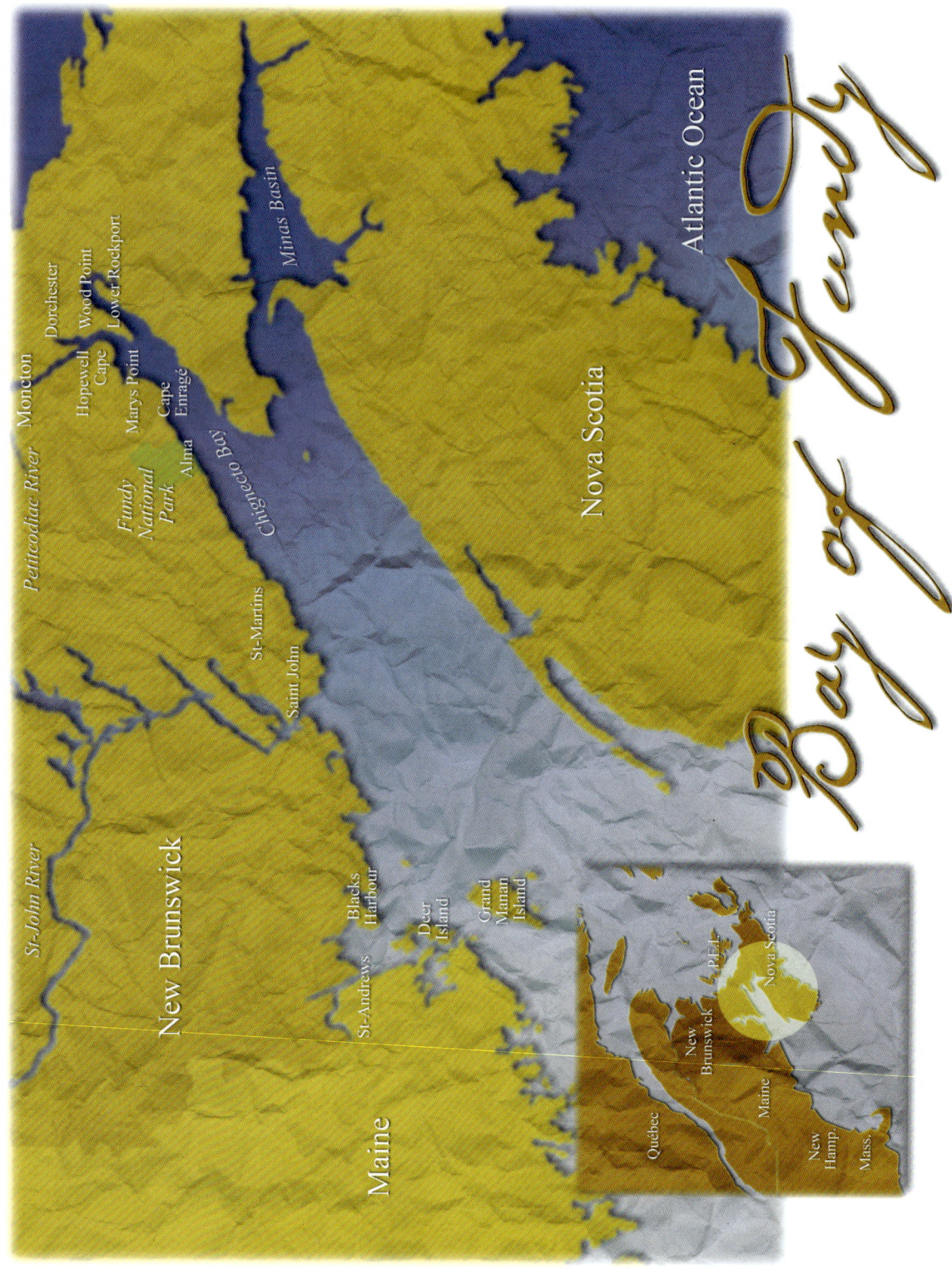

Shells, starfish, sparkling stones and of course plenty of mud provide hours of entertainment for children at Cape Enrage.

The Magical Bay of Fundy

Pulsing with giant tides, resounding with the cry of sea gulls, and surrounded by majestic cliffs, the Bay of Fundy can cast a spell on those who come to visit.

A narrow arm of the Atlantic Ocean, the bay reaches deep into the land as if trying to touch Prince Edward Island. It separates the provinces of New Brunswick and Nova Scotia, and towards its upper end splits into two basins, Chignecto Bay and Minas Basin. From there, its tidal waters enter smaller bays and inlets, carrying their salty content into rivers and creeks and over mudflats and marshes.

GEOLOGY

Fundy lies in a rift valley formed about 300 million years ago, but the bay as we know it now is much more recent—perhaps several million years old. Its predominantly rocky shores tell of a long geological history.

It is hard to imagine that hundreds of millions of years ago this area was covered with tropical vegetation and inhabited by now extinct animals. Crumbling cliffs along the bay have slowly uncovered fossil beds that tell of those times. A variety of these fossilized trees, plants and animals can be seen in the New Brunswick Museum in Saint John.

The tide and wave action of the bay sculpts the soft sandstone of the cliffs—but these are not the only forces at work. In winter, the many cracks and crevices fill with water, which freezes and expands, flaking off layers of stone that leave wondrous shapes on the shore.

THE TIDES

The pulse of the Fundy tides, repeated for thousands of years, has created a special world for nature and for humans. The constant ebb and flow influences the weather, the climate, the plants and animals of sea, shore and land, and even the plans of travellers whose aim is to visit the bay's impressive sites.

To a visitor unaccustomed to large tides, it can be quite astounding to see the waters of the bay a kilometre from shore or a nearly empty river bed, then a few hours later observe from the same spot, the ocean waves pounding on the beach or the river brimming full.

THE TIDES—WHY AND HOW?

A landlubber might wonder why the times of high and low tide change from day to day, and why the height of the tidal bore varies from impressive to disappointing.

The phenomenon of the tides is complicated, related as it is to the two heavenly bodies, the moon and the sun, that exert a noticeable force on the earth's waters. As the earth turns, their gravitational pull causes the ocean waters to rise and fall on our shores. The size of the tides depends on the phase of the moon and the distance of the moon and sun from the earth.

The timing of Fundy tides is controlled mainly by the moon, which is why the tide is almost an hour later each day. While the earth rotates once in 24 hours, the moon advances in its orbit, and it takes an extra 52 minutes for the earth to catch up and be in the same relative position.

But why are Fundy tides so large? It's because of the shape and the size of the bay. The tides are forced to greater and greater heights as they travel up the progressively narrower and shallower bay. In addition, the length and depth of the bay are such that its waters naturally oscillate not only at the same time but for the same length of time as do the lunar tides. Thus reinforced, the largest tides can climb to 6 stories high (16 metres, 54 feet). The average tidal range increases up the bay from 5 metres at Grand Manan to 7 metres at Saint John and more than 10 metres at Hopewell Cape.

Although spectacular, the tide generally does not arrive with a great swoosh, engulfing everything in its path. Instead it moves slowly and steadily. And so, twice daily the tides leave great stretches of ocean bottom devoid of water. A few hours later, however, the river estuaries are brimming with water and fishing boats are bobbing beside wharves where earlier they lay stranded on the bottom.

There are many locations along the coast of the Bay of Fundy where one can view the tidal changes and watch with fascination the water slowly mounting rocky shores, rushing up muddy creeks and rivers, or creeping across mudflats and marshes. Equally intriguing is to see the water slowly descend, leaving behind glistening beds of seaweed and deposits of wet mud.

In some places the tides show themselves in special ways, so they attract many spectators. Thus, on the Petitcodiac River, at Moncton and Riverview, one can watch the tide arrive as a tidal bore, a wave of water that rushes up the river accompanied by swirling flocks of sea gulls, eager to swoop on morsels of food stirred up by the turbulence.

In Saint John, the tides cause a waterfall to change direction! The majestic St. John River enters the Bay of Fundy through a rocky gorge, its waters cascading down to join the ocean. At high tide, however, the bay becomes higher than the river, reversing the flow, and the famous Reversing Falls rapids churn inland.

The ebb and flow of Fundy's huge tides drive powerful currents in the bay. They are particularly impressive in passages among the islands of Passamaquoddy Bay. There, off the park at the southern end of Deer Island, The Old Sow, a large tidal whirlpool, can be dangerous for small boats when the tide is running strong. Remarkable currents can also be seen from the Deer Island ferry.

WEATHER

Fog, whether thin bands that accent the coastal scenery or thick banks that almost obliterate any view of it, is a common feature of Fundy weather. In spring and summer, warm, humid air moving off the land is cooled by the bay. In winter, extremely cold air can cool the moister air over the bay and cause sea smoke, wispy vapours that rise like smoke from the bay. These temperature differences are accentuated by the tremendous tidal mixing that slows the warming of the bay in summer and its cooling in winter.

CLIMATE AND MARSHES

In a profound way, the tides also influence the natural life of the Fundy region. The cool and moist climate creates a lush and fast-growing forest with a great variety of mammals and birds. In some locations around the bay, the oncoming tide covered vast stretches of surrounding lowlands with salt water. Following the arrival of European settlers, many of those marshes were drained for agricultural use. The resulting dykelands are renowned for the quantity and quality of their hay, on which many hundreds of cattle still pasture each summer.

Today, an attempt is being made to save what remains of the tidal marshes because they play such a vital role in the bay's productivity. The marshes grow salt-tolerant vegetation and harbour unique animal life. Some of the salt marsh plants—goose-tongue greens and samphire—have been favourite foods of the locals for generations. Each summer they are gathered, then savoured as vegetables and pickled for the winter.

BIRDS

The tides have created particularly favorable habitat for migrating shorebirds. The vast mudflats exposed at low tide are a feeding ground for millions of tiny, graceful shorebirds which take advantage of the sea life (worms and crustaceans) that lives below the surface of the mud. The Bay of Fundy

An insignificant disturbance sends a cloud of semi-palmated sandpipers into an aerial frenzy, swooping in each direction above the beaches at Marys Point—a protected bird sanctuary.

is one of few places in the world where shorebirds congregate in such great numbers. Birdwatchers from all over the world come to witness this spectacle in August. Mary's Point, Johnsons Mills and Hopewell Cape are the best places. Only at high tide do the birds appear on the beaches to rest on the sand while they wait for the mudflats to be exposed again. When gathering in enormous flocks, they perform awe-inspiring flights.

There are many other birds which use the Bay of Fundy as a migration route during their journey north or south. Grand Manan Island is a natural place for migrating birds to land and rest after flying for hours over the water. Here, too, seabirds not often seen from land can be found over the ocean or nesting on isolated islets. Such unique birds as Atlantic puffins, razorbills and arctic terns raise their young on Machias Seal Island, a tiny rocky island with restricted visitation.

A humpback whale lifts its tail and observes a group of very excited creatures called tourists snapping pictures before it disappears beneath the waves.

WHALES

Each summer the mouth of the bay, especially around Grand Manan, becomes a gathering place of the giants. Whales of several species play, court and feed in these productive, turbulent waters. Porpoises, dolphins and seals also take advantage of the rich feeding grounds.

Of the whales, the right whale is in danger of becoming extinct. The reason for its tragic decline stems from the fact that it produced great quantities of oil and was easy to hunt (hence, it was the "right whale" to kill). Nowadays they are completely protected. These friendly denizens of the sea are curious and playful, readily approached by boats, sometimes even putting on a show for the people on board. When courting, which they do frequently in the Bay of Fundy, they are so involved in their amorous activities they can be oblivious to the spectators around them.

HISTORY

The bay has borne various names. The Passamaquoddy Indians called it "Bakudabakek," meaning sea lake. Entering the bay in 1604, French explorers Champlain and Sieur de Monts named it "Baye françoise." The present-day name may come from the Portuguese *fondo*, meaning deep, or, more likely, from the French word *fendu*, meaning split, probably in reference to a prominent split cape or the split in the upper bay.

Legend tells how the northeastern part of the bay got its name. Fog lifting from the tidal marshes often hangs like gossamer veils on the crown of a prominent mountain. Upon seeing that beautiful sight, Champlain is said to have exclaimed, "chapeau de Dieu" (cap of God), so the bay and the mountain became "Chipoudy" and eventually "Shepody." The Mi'kmaq who lived in the area had called the local river "Esedabit," also a likely origin for "Shepody."

Here, Glooscap, the Mi'kmaq legendary friend and protector, left giant footprints on those shores. In places along the coast, Indian tribes once had their encampments. Traces of middens filled with sea shells and animal bones indicate that they fished, hunted and gathered food along the shore and on the islands. Grand Manan Island was known to them as Munanook (big island).

Passamaquoddy Bay, embraced by Deer Island, Campobello and many smaller islands, was the main area of the Passamaquoddy tribe. The St. Croix River, which flows into that bay, is the border between Canada and the USA. Champlain and Sieur de Monts spent their first winter in Canada on St. Croix Island in the river. Almost half of their party died from scurvy and the rigours of that winter of 1604-05. The following year they moved to Port Royal in the Annapolis Valley of Nova Scotia. Port Royal dominated the Bay of Fundy for many years. There, the first Acadian settlers arrived and then spread to establish other communities around the bay.

COMMUNITIES

Champlain was not the first to visit the bay from overseas. Fishing and whaling drew the first Europeans. Explorers followed, in time bringing wave after wave of settlers. The Acadians, who settled the bay shores, made friends with Indians, built dykes to hold back the sea water from coastal marshes, and established small, thriving communities. The fertile marshlands surrounding the bay and the plentiful fish and wildlife made them prosper.

After about 150 years, distant wars, treaties and the changing fortunes of European rulers disrupted the lives of those peaceful people. In 1755 a new English governor demanded that the Acadians swear allegiance to England, which they declined to do. Many were deported while others fled to northern New Brunswick and Quebec. Following the expulsion of the Acadians, English settlers trickled into the area until 1783 when a major influx of Loyalists arrived after the American Revolution. They established Saint John, St. Andrews and many smaller communities. To this day, the resort town of St. Andrews-by-the-Sea bears the mark of its Loyalist heritage.

The English, German, Irish and Scottish settlers who followed were farmers, fishermen, lumberjacks, sailors, cobblers, stone-masons, and shipbuilders. It took much work and pioneer effort to secure the dykelands again. Slowly they developed busy communities along the bay, which became an artery for travel and commerce with the whole world. Lumbering, shipping, sailing and the building of wooden vessels became important industries.

FISHERY

Today every convenient harbour on the Bay of Fundy is used for sheltering fishing fleets—a colourful assemblage of lobster boats, scallop draggers and seiners—crowded at wharves and surrounded by fish plants, smoke houses, long rows of stacked traps and buoys, and piles of nets.

In the beginning, great quantities of cod, salmon, and shad (all rather scarce today) were of most interest to the fishermen. Later, herring, smoked and canned, were sent to European and West Indian markets. Today lobsters and scallops are popular exports. The newest fishery, aquaculture, employs large floating cages placed in sheltered waters to raise salmon for the market.

An ingenious way of catching large schools of herring using weirs has been practiced for generations in the outer bay. Weirs are circular enclosures of pilings pounded into the sea bottom with nets strung around them. Each weir (pronounced either weer or ware) has a name such as Cora Belle, The Goose, The Plumper, and Night Hawk.

An interesting food item that grows on rocky shores and is exposed at low tide is a unique purplish seaweed called dulse. It has been enjoyed by the locals for many years and is now marketed farther afield. Dulse tastes of salt, sea, and fish, a curious combination rich in vitamins and minerals that takes some getting used to.

FISHERMEN

Most of the fishermen come from families that have followed the sea for generations. They invest into their boats not only money but also pride and hope for a lifelong occupation. Their life is demanding, often exhausting and sometimes hazardous, but nevertheless very rewarding.

A visit to a cemetery can reveal a lot about the fortunes of those people. Inscriptions tell of natural disasters, fire, and epidemics, of women dying in childbirth, of children struck by diphtheria or scarlet fever, of men lost at sea. A monument erected in memory of the victims of a tragic shipwreck brings out stories from old-timers.

The Maritimes' traditional building material was the readily obtainable wood, which was easy to work with, durable and warm. Houses, boats and

Destination Fundy Trail

Bluish green and muddy brown are the two colours that the Bay of Fundy waters provide for kayakers and beachgoers at St. Martin.

wharves had their beginning in the nearby forest. The predominant colour of homes, churches and boats is white. Photographers and painters are enchanted by the charms of the coastal villages.

Visitors often comment on the friendliness and hospitality of Maritimers. There is a sense of community, a great feeling of belonging and pride in those who have lived here all their lives, but they are eager to share and be helpful to strangers to make their visit enjoyable and memorable. Those qualities entice artisans, artists, and writers to settle along the shores of the Bay of Fundy to enjoy the friendliness of people as well as the beauty of the countryside.

A prominent part of the seascape is the lighthouses and their associated foghorns. Erected on headlands and islands to protect and warn those at sea, they were the life-saving stations and shining beacons of hope. Lighthouse keepers and their families often became heroes whose lives and deeds are immortalized in poems and stories, such as "Sand Reef Light" by Grace Helen Mowat:

SAND REEF LIGHT

The lighthouse on the sand reef is like a friend to me,
That sends out little friendly beams across the twilight sea
Beyond the distant seine-reel, beyond the herring weir,
When day draws on to evening, I see its light appear.
When winds through bird forsaken trees and lifeless branches sound,

When damp and dead the garden growth lies rotting on the ground,
When early autumn shadows fall across the wind-swept sea,
I watch to see the sand reef send out its light to me.
When crows from barren stubble fields fly home against the sky,
When from the lonely tract of sand, I hear the sea gulls cry,
I stand beside the window, till through the gathering night,
I catch again the friendly gleam of my lone sand reef light.

Today, aside from Machias Seal Island, all lighthouses in the bay are automated. Serviced by helicopters, they are reminders of a bygone era. Visiting a lighthouse, one can muse about what it would be like to be there during a vicious storm.

TOURISM

Today, tourism has become an important element of the Fundy economy. The tides, scenery, wildlife and the fishing communities of the bay attract many visitors.

The Tantramar Marsh at the head of the bay was the largest of all Fundy's tidal marshes. The name Tantramar comes from a French word meaning 'a great noise,' which refers to the many thousands of geese and ducks that gathered there before it was drained and turned into agricultural land. Today, the marsh is a beautiful, great stretch of grassland that has inspired many poets and artists. In the charming university town of Sackville, a sample of the former abundance of wetland birds is found in the Sackville Waterfowl Park.

Near the very head of the bay, the Hopewell Rocks are one of the bay's natural wonders. Tide, wave and frost action have sculpted the sandstone into intriguing shapes: huge rocky sentinels standing on the shore. There, at low tide, one can wander amongst the seaweed-encrusted rocks and peek into small caves, or, watching from above at high tide, see the islets surrounded by the sea—giant "flowerpots" topped with trees and shrubs.

Fundy National Park is a perfect spot to witness the oncoming tides and admire the height of the incoming water by watching the ascent or descent of colourful fishing boats at the wharf in Alma. The park was established to protect a special area along the Fundy coast. It has beautiful views, many trails and an interpretive program that highlights the Fundy shore.

A bit farther down the bay, the Fundy Trail Parkway is a popular drive with great vistas along the rugged shore east of St. Martins. It provides access to a coastal hiking trail that connects with the Fundy Park trail system, and thence via the Dobson Trail all the way to Moncton.

On the west side of the industrial city of Saint John, the privately established Irving Nature Park is a peninsula jutting into the sea, with well-maintained trails and views of rocky cliffs, a beach and salt marsh. Farther down the bay, a lovely provincial park centres on the sands of New River Beach and an adjacent rocky headland.

The three largest islands at the mouth of the bay are all working fishing communities with scenic harbours and rugged coastlines. The largest, Grand Manan, is very popular with tourists. Campobello, once the summer home of former U.S. President Franklin Delano Roosevelt, is home to an international park named in his memory, as well as a provincial park. Deer Island retains more of a traditional character.

Why is the Bay of Fundy so special? Perhaps because of its long history, perhaps because of its rugged beauty or because of the life teaming in its waters, but most of all because of its giant tides, an awe-inspiring phenomenon before which we stand in realization of how small we are in the scheme of things.

Mary Majka and David Christie

Destination Fundy Trail

With twilight approaching, the lighthouse at Cape Enrage twinkles a beam out over the Bay of Fundy, maintaining its nightly vigil. The lighthouse here at Cape Enrage has been in operation since 1838. Both the lighthouse and the lightkeeper's residence were restored by high school students from nearby Moncton. In summer the lightkeeper's house doubles as a restaurant that serves some of the best blueberry pie and ice cream this side of the Maritimes.

Facing Page: At Letete near Deer Island, the sun burns through the fog to reveal long fields of varech exposed by the low tide.

Destination Fundy Trail

An opening in a white picket fence leads to a world of adventure at Cape Enrage, where the sheer cliffs that reach heights of over 150 feet are the training grounds for those learning the art of rappelling. Cape Enrage is a stack of vertical cliffs and rocky gorges perched high above Chignecto Bay and facing Nova Scotia. It has a wild, rugged beauty and a solitude that mesmerizes the soul.

Destination Fundy Trail

Mother Nature creates a Van Gogh-like masterpiece in Fundy Park.

Overleaf: A sea of sunflowers basking in the sun stretches toward a clear blue sky near St. Joseph.

Destination Fundy Trail

A sunlit veil of morning mist over Fundy.

Destination Fundy Trail

A puffin stands alone on a cliff, enshrouded by fog. The bay offers a multitude of delicacies for this bird during the summer months, including capelan and sand eel.

Destination Fundy Trail

Destination Fundy Trail

A blazing sunset descends towards the v-shaped gap in a promontory across from Cape Enrage, known locally as "the Split."

Facing Page: At the end of a long, rainy day, a fog patch rolls out past the coast and cliffs of North Head on Grand Manan.

Destination Fundy Trail

Destination Fundy Trail

A reflection of bulrushes and reeds by the pond at Fundy park headquarters creates a tranquil setting for the nature lover.

Facing Page: After a long walk along a trail in southwest Fundy Park, a young couple finds serenity beside these splendid cascades.

Destination Fundy Trail

Low tide at Alma Harbour keeps boats snug and safe from the tides and swirls of the sea.

Facing Page: The rich, nutrient-abundant waters of Fundy reflect a lighthouse in the early morning hours.

Destination Fundy Trail

A multitude of tiny dew droplets clinging to a spider's web is a common sight, especially if one is camping in Fundy Park and rises early.

Facing Page: A small stream in Fundy National Park offers its cool water to the surrounding moss and ferns.

Destination Fundy Trail

Destination Fundy Trail

Supported by an intricate array of wooden stilts, this weathered fishing shed in Grand Manan's main community of North Head shows how high the tides in the Bay of Fundy can climb. The name Grand Manan originates from the Maliseet word "man-an-ook," meaning "the island."

Facing Page: The Point Wolfe covered bridge in Fundy National Park crosses a riverbed struck by an unusual dry spell.

Destination Fundy Trail

The rolling green hills of Lower Rockport, where the Bay of Fundy is hemmed in by wheat fields and marshlands that descend to the shoreline.

Facing Page: A tractor rests in a field near Sussex before the arrival of the farmer and a full day of harvesting.

Overleaf: In a bay at Cape Enrage, high tide once again covers the marshland and gives life to a multitude of small organisms belonging to the phytoplankton and zoo plankton kingdom, which in turn sustain larger organisms such as birds, fish and mammals—the cycle of life in the Bay of Fundy.

Destination Fundy Trail

A single blade of grass breaks through the mud-caked banks of the Petitcodiac River near Moncton

Facing Page: East Quoddy Head lighthouse basks in a golden sunset. Located at the north end of Campobello Island, this monument is accessible for only a short time at low tide. Beware...if you linger too long (as I did) you'll have to wade through two or more feet of water.

23

Destination Fundy Trail

An old fishing settlement on Grand Manan, Seal Cove emerges from the fog.

Facing Page: Stones polished by the high tides carpet the shoreline at Cape Enrage, while the horizon reveals the red cliffs of Nova Scotia on the other side of the Bay of Fundy.

Destination Fundy Trail

At Bennett Lake, lily pads provide a resting place for small insects—
but beware of the hungry frogs that also inhabit the pristine lake.

Facing Page: At the mouth of Big Salmon River, pieces of wood mark
the location of an old wharf. Nearby, hiking trails crisscross the land
offering panoramic views from high cliffs.

Destination Fundy Trail

Destination Fundy Trail

The scattered remains of a dyke or aboiteau near Wood Point is covered in a chocolate-coloured coating of famous Fundy mud. These aboiteau were used by the early settlers to prevent saltwater from the bay from flooding the agriculturally rich marshlands.

Destination Fundy Trail

The tidal flats of the Petitcodiac River in Moncton create what is known as a tidal bore. Each day with the powerful surging tides, the sea pushes its way against the downstream force of the river creating the phenomenon called a wave pulse, which can reach a height of 2-12 inches. It's definitely not boring!

Destination Fundy Trail

Destination Fundy Trail

Mosquito Lake in Fundy National Park offers an ideal spot for observing moose in their natural habitat. The lake owes its name to the abundance of mosquitoes in the area.

Facing Page: As night falls, the Swallowtail Lighthouse in Grand Manan offers a guiding light to mariners. Below the light, a fishing trap is awaiting a school of herring that follows the island's shoreline.

Destination Fundy Trail

The Bay of Fundy is considered one of the last coastal wildernesses in North America. Wild and unspoiled, it is home to geese, deer, great herons, moose, beaver, porcupines, coyotes and even peregrine falcons. The original inhabitants of the park lands were the Mi'kmaq and the Maliseet.

Destination Fundy Trail

The Flower Pot Islands slowly emerge with the receding tide. Grass, flowers, shrubs and trees that inhabit the tops of these peculiarly shaped monoliths give them their characteristic name. Varech that grows along the sides of the islands provide a clue as to the height the sea rises to at high tide.

Destination Fundy Trail

Destination Fundy Trail

The saltwater marshlands on the way to Cape Enrage are periodically engorged with the high tide of Fundy. They are thousands of shades of green and gold.

Facing Page: Near Gardner Creek, bales of hay and fireweed announce summertime along Fundy Bay.

Overleaf: At Cape Enrage, an old spruce's profile is silhouetted against the sunrise and the Bay of Fundy.

Destination Fundy Trail